Section 1)   Introduction

During the depths of the 2007-2009 housing crisis, media stories documented the deteriorating conditions in many cities and neighborhoods overwhelmed by foreclosures. Older, central city neighborhoods, particularly in Ohio and Michigan, saw entire city blocks become largely vacant (ElBoghdady 2007, Kotlowitz 2009). Scavengers stripped fixtures and copper pipes from empty houses. The vacant shells attracted criminal activity and squatters. Sprawling exurban subdivisions – most notably in Arizona, California, Florida and Nevada - were arrested halfway through construction, ghost towns of partly built structures and vacant lots (Roth 2008, Shapiro 2008). Moving beyond anecdotal accounts in the media, a growing academic literature has documented the negative impacts of foreclosures on nearby property values and surrounding neighborhoods (see, for instance, Campbell, Giglio and Pathak 2011; Ellen, Lacoe and Sharygin 2011; Gerardi, Lambie-Hanson and Willen 2012; Hartley 2010; Immergluck and Smith 2006; Lin, Rosenblatt and Yao 2009; Mian, Sufi and Trebbi 2011; Schuetz, Been and Ellen 2009). Hypothesized mechanisms of negative externalities include creating visual blight, attracting crime and antisocial activity, and sending negative signals about the neighborhood's future to current residents and potential investors. Addressing problems associated with neighborhood blight are typically the responsibility of local government agencies: police and fire departments, building code inspectors and tax assessors. However, the scale of the housing crisis exceeded the resources of many local governments, a problem exacerbated by the drop in property tax revenues caused by foreclosures.

To provide assistance to local communities severely affected by the crisis, Congress adopted a series of programs knowns as the Neighborhood Stabilization Program (NSP). The three rounds of funding, known colloquially as NSP1, NSP2 and NSP3, provided a total of about

1

$7 billion to state and local governments.[1] NSP was intended to mitigate the impact of foreclosures on neighborhoods by reducing the stock of distressed properties, removing visual blight and sites of crime, and signaling to residents that the neighborhood was capable of improvement (Joice 2011). Similar to the Community Development Block Grant (CDBG) program, NSP was structured as grants from the U.S. Department of Housing and Urban Development (HUD) to state and local governments and qualified non-profits. Grantees could use the funds for five specific activities: rehabilitation or redevelopment of foreclosed and vacant properties, demolition of blighted structures, land banking, and stand-alone financing for purchase or development of affordable housing. Neighborhoods (defined as census tracts) were eligible to receive investments based on the initial economic and housing market conditions, especially the prevalence of foreclosed and vacant properties. NSP was the largest public policy effort to address the impact of foreclosures on neighborhoods, and was a substantial influx of resources for many local communities.[2]

This paper presents evidence about how grantees targeted their investments from the second round of NSP funding (NSP2), what initial housing market conditions prevailed in NSP2 tracts, and how housing markets changed in NSP2 tracts during the program's implementation period, relative to other tracts in the same counties. As its name implies, NSP's goal was to improve housing markets at the neighborhood level, therefore assessing changing conditions in NSP2 tracts is an important step in evaluating the program's effectiveness. Several studies have documented difficulties faced by grantees in implementing all three rounds of NSP (Fraser and

---

[1] The first round of funding, NSP1, provided $3.9 billion as part of the Housing and Economic Recovery Act of 2008. The second round, totaling $2 billion, was part of the 2009 American Recovery and Reinvestment Act. The third round of $1 billion was issued under the 2010 Dodd-Frank Wall Street Reform and Consumer Protection Act (HUD 2010).
[2] NSP's funding is much smaller than other housing market recovery programs, such as the Home Affordable Modification Program, the Troubled Assed Relief Program and the homebuyer tax credits (see Been et al 2011, Immergluck 2012, Gerardi et al 2011).

Oakley 2015, Immergluck 2012, Newburger 2010, Nickerson 2010, Reid 2011). In particular, they note the challenges of acquiring foreclosed and REO properties in targeted locations and the bureaucratic hurdles that slowed down the process of rehabbing and re-occupying distressed properties. They also point out that, for the most severely affected communities, the amount of NSP funding provided was modest relative to the number of distressed properties.

Only a few studies to date have documented neighborhood outcomes in NSP treated areas. Schuetz et al (2015) examine long-run housing market trends in NSP2 tracts and other low-value tracts across 19 counties. They find that NSP2 tracts were initially more distressed than average tracts, but followed similar housing market trajectories during the recovery period. Ergungor and Nelson (2012) examined vacancy rates of former REO properties purchased with NSP funds to vacancy rates of comparable former REOs, not funded by NSP, in Cuyahoga County. They find that, in neighborhoods targeted by the first round of NSP, properties purchased by individuals (i.e. presumed owner-occupants) are less likely to be vacant. They find no significant difference in vacancy rates among NSP2-targeted areas, although during their study period, very few NSP2 properties had completed rehabilitation. Graves and Shuey (2013) conduct a small scale, mostly qualitative analysis of changes in social conditions around properties in Boston that were rehabbed using NSP funding. The authors find that only half of the eight NSP properties in their studied had begun or completed renovation as of 2012, while seven of the eight control properties (also previously vacant REOs) had been rehabbed. Somewhat surprisingly, the authors learned through interviews that most neighbors of REO properties were not aware of the previous foreclosures, and did not perceive the vacant homes as significant disamenities. However, the small sample size and Boston's strong housing market, relative to most NSP grantees, make it difficult to extrapolate from these results.

In another light, NSP is the latest in a long history of place-based policies aimed at removing urban blight and revitalizing neighborhoods, from urban renewal programs of the 1940-1960s to HOPE VI in the 1990s. Compared to these prior policies, NSP is somewhat unusual in that it targeted mostly privately-owned single-family detached housing in largely owner-occupied neighborhoods. Moreover, although place-based policies generally target distressed neighborhoods, none except NSP have occurred during a nationwide housing slump of such magnitude or duration. Empirical research on the effects of these programs – especially HOPE VI -- on neighborhood economic conditions has produced mixed results (see, for instance, Abt Associates 2003; Griswold et al 2014; Zielenbach and Voith 2010; Pooley 2014; Jacobs 1961, Wilson 1963, Teaford 2010). No consistent patterns are observable from these studies on housing market outcomes such as housing prices, vacancies, and crime rates. Previous studies have also found mixed results from policies that fund or undertake development and/or rehabilitation of affordable housing, such as Federal public housing, Low Income Housing Tax Credits (LIHTC), and the Community Development Block Grant program (CDBG) (Baum-Snow and Marion 2009; Ellen et al 2007; Ellen and Voicu 2006; Galster et al 2004; Pooley 2014; Schwartz et al 2006; Smith and Hevener 2011). These studies vary in geographic area and methodology as well as programs studied, making it difficult to draw consistent conclusions about the effectiveness of publicly-funded housing rehabilitation.

This study presents the first multi-city quantitative analysis of how NSP2 investments were targeted and how NSP2-treated neighborhoods have fared during the housing recovery. We use data collected from NSP2 grantees on the location, type, and timing of their investments to assess whether census tracts that received NSP2 investments experienced stronger housing market outcomes than comparable tracts in the same counties. The study focuses on seven large urban counties—Cook IL, Cuyahoga OH, Los Angeles CA, Maricopa AZ, Miami-Dade FL, Philadelphia PA, and Wayne MI—which represent diverse underlying housing markets and where grantees used different strategies to implement NSP2. We estimate reduced-form regressions on the change in several housing market outcomes (distressed properties, vacancies and sales volume) as a function of NSP2 investment. Because NSP2 was targeted at initially distressed areas, which might be expected to have weak recoveries, selection of appropriate comparison groups is important to understand the likely trajectory of NSP2 tracts in the absence of the program. We identify two sets of tracts that did not receive NSP2 but would likely have faced weak recoveries based on initial conditions: tracts that previously received other housing subsidies (CDBG, HOME, LIHTC and NSP1) and tracts below median county income.

Results indicate that grantees' approaches to NSP2, characterized by the type of activity and targeted locations, varied across counties. Grantees in Cuyahoga and Wayne Counties focused primarily on demolition and land-banking. Rehab and redevelopment dominated NSP2 activity in Los Angeles, Maricopa and Miami. Grantees in Cook and Philadelphia pursued mixed strategies. The median NSP2 tract received about three properties and $400,000 dollars – quite small compared to the housing stock and scale of distress – but the size of NSP2 investments also varied widely. The selection of NSP2 tracts is correlated with initial housing market characteristics, such as the frequency of distressed and/or vacant properties, as well as demographic characteristics.[3] Tracts that had previously received other housing subsidies through CDBG, HOME, LIHTC or NSP1 were more likely to be selected for NSP2 investments.

Housing recovery proceeded unevenly among NSP2 tracts during the program's implementation period, and the evidence linking NSP2 activity to housing changes is quite mixed. NSP2 tracts in all counties saw substantial decreases in the inventory of distressed

---

[3] Di et al (2010) also find clustering of mortgage assistance programs in low-value neighborhoods.

properties, as fewer properties entered foreclosure and the stock of REO properties declined. Changes in vacancy rates and sales volume varied more across counties. NSP2 expenditures in Cuyahoga County were correlated with stronger recovery, measured by smaller increases in vacancy and smaller decreases in sales volume. Results also suggest that NSP2 spending in Los Angeles was positively correlated with growth in sales volume, generally a sign of a strengthening market. In Cook County, NSP2 activity was correlated with larger vacancy increases. In the remaining four counties, there is no consistent evidence that NSP2 activity is associated with differential housing recovery. The small scale of NSP2 investments at the census tract level may explain the program's apparently limited impacts. Future research should investigate whether NSP2 may have had impacts at a smaller geographic scale or in selected locations within counties.

The remainder of this paper is organized as follows. Section 2 discusses the NSP2 data collection and presents descriptive statistics on county- and tract-level investments. Section 3 outlines the empirical strategy and additional data sources. Section 4 presents empirical results; Section 5 outlines next steps and conclusions.

Section 2)   NSP2 background

The analysis focuses on the second round of funding, NSP2, which was designed to correct some limitations of the first round of funding and was the subject of a formal evaluation by HUD. NSP1 was allocated to state and local governments via an automatic funding formula, and resulted in widespread dispersion of small amounts of investment. By contrast, NSP2 was awarded based on competitive applications, with grantees encouraged to concentrate their investments in a few targeted neighborhoods at sufficient scale to improve housing market outcomes (Joice 2011). Applicants had to specify the type and expected quantity of activities (i.e. number of properties to be rehabbed or demolished) and list the census tracts in which they planned to invest. The range of allowed activities gave grantees flexibility to tailor their strategies to local housing market conditions, so that grantees could pursue different strategies in different cities (Reid 2011). Like other components of the Federal stimulus program, NSP2 funds were required to be spent quickly, with 100 percent of funds expended by February 2013.

2.1)   Data collection

The data used in this analysis were collected during an evaluation of NSP2 commissioned by HUD, which concluded in June 2014 (one year after the expenditure deadline). Property-level information on the location, type, timing, and expenditures on NSP2 investments were collected from 28 grantees across 19 counties. The counties were selected to provide a diversity of underlying housing markets, to include grantees with very large NSP2 awards (overall and predicted per-census tract), and oversampled states with high incidence of financially distressed properties. For the current study, we focus on the seven largest counties, because they have enough tracts that received NSP2 investment to allow within-county analysis at the census tract level. The seven counties also vary by housing market conditions and implementation strategies, discussed below. Table 1 shows the counties included in the study.

Standardized information reported by grantees for every NSP2 property include the address, type(s) of activities undertaken, beginning and (if relevant) ending dates of intervention, and the amount of NSP2 funds expended.[4] For a smaller subset of properties, information was provided on the structure type and number of units in structure, intermediate activity dates, and

---

[4] For rehab/redevelopment, the first date is the date of acquisition, the last date is the disposal (sale) of the completed property. Many of the demolitions were conducted without the grantee acquiring the property, so starting and ending dates refer to the demolition activity. Some rehabbed and land-banked properties were still held by the grantee at the end of the study period.

property tenure before and after NSP2. No information is available on properties' physical conditions either at purchase or completion.

2.2) Descriptive statistics on NSP2 investments

Collectively, the seven counties received over $700 million of NSP2 funds (about 35 percent of the national total) and treated about 4800 properties (Table 1). But the scale of NSP2 investment varied widely across counties. Los Angeles County received the largest amount of funds, about $220 million, allocated to six grantee organizations who operated in twelve separate jurisdictions, including the cities of Los Angeles and Long Beach. The smallest monetary allocation was to the Cuyahoga County Land Reutilization Corporation, a non-profit organization that acquired properties in Cleveland and five smaller cities in Cuyahoga County. In all but two counties, at least one public agency and one non-profit organization received NSP2 funds. Generally the grantees targeted different geographic areas within the county, either focusing on separate political jurisdictions or different neighborhoods within the largest city, to avoid competing to acquire the same properties. Besides Cuyahoga, Wayne County was the only county with a single grantee: the Michigan State Housing Department, which oversaw all NSP2 activity throughout the state. While the public agencies only operated in their home jurisdiction, some of the non-profits were aligned with large, national organizations that worked in multiple states. For instance, affiliates of Chicanos Por La Causa worked in Chicago, Los Angeles, Phoenix and Philadelphia. Interviews conducted with grantees during the evaluation revealed that many grantees took different approaches to implementing NSP2 even when performing ostensibly the same tasks. For example, among grantees conducting rehabilitation, some aimed for decent but modest quality internal finishes, while others used higher quality and more costly building materials or appliances.

Output levels – the number of properties treated with NSP2 funds – and cost per property also varied considerably across counties. Some of this reflects differences in activities (Table 2). Wayne and Cuyahoga focused on demolition/land banking, while the three Sand State Counties (Los Angeles, Maricopa and Miami-Dade) primarily conducted rehab or redevelopment. Demolition was substantially less costly per property, enabling Wayne and Cuyahoga to treat larger numbers of properties. Cook County treated the smallest number of properties at the highest per-property cost; about 42 percent of the rehabbed properties in Chicago were multifamily structures, compared to fewer than five percent in other counties doing rehab.[5] The difference in activity costs is reflected in Table 2. For instance, in Philadelphia, about 42 percent of treated properties were rehabbed, but rehab accounted for nearly 86 percent of total NSP2 spending. Stand-alone financing was used quite rarely by grantees in these seven counties; almost all the financing in Los Angeles County was done by a single non-profit organization that made loans to another non-profit affordable housing developer. For a small share of properties, grantees used NSP2 funds for multiple activities on the same property, meaning that both rehab/redevelopment and demolition/land-banking were reported.[6] Interviews with grantees suggest that in some of these cases, grantees purchased properties with the intent to rehabilitate them but because of poor physical conditions, could not afford the rehab work so demolished the structure instead.

---

[5] There is ongoing research to explore more systematically factors behind variation in costs and output across grantees and jurisdictions.

[6] The NSP2 RFP lists five separate activities, but for purposes of this analysis, they are collapsed into three categories. Rehab and redevelopment both result in the presence of a newly renovated housing structure on the parcel, and so will look similar to external viewers (neighbors or potential investors). Similarly, demolition and land-banking result in a vacant structure or lot. Financing could be used as down-payment assistance to low-income homebuyers purchasing an existing structure (not one rehabbed through NSP2), or as development finance for new affordable housing (not carried out by the NSP2 grantee). Properties that reported having NSP2 funds for financing in conjunction with rehab/redevelopment are classified as rehab/redevelopment for purposes of this study.

For purposes of this analysis, census tracts are used as the definition of neighborhoods. HUD's initial eligibility criteria were calculated for tracts, and grantees were required to identify specific tracts in which they intended to work. Table 3 shows the median number of treated tracts, tract-level scale of NSP2 investment for each county. Combining all seven counties, 648 census tracts received some NSP2 investment, with a median of three properties and under $400,000 per tract. The median number of housing units per NSP2 treated tract is about 1500, so NSP2 was a relatively small scale intervention in most tracts. As with the county-level summary, however, the tract-level size and scale of intervention varied across counties. The median NSP2 tract in Los Angeles had only two NSP2 properties, while Wayne County tracts had a median of 14 properties. Housing values vary widely across tracts within and across counties. To give a better sense of the scale of NSP2 expenditures per tract, the last column in Table 3 shows tract NSP2 spending divided by the tract median housing value (taken from the 2005-2009 ACS). These values also reflect differences in activities; for instance, Chicago's relatively high score of 9.7 reflects the acquisition of multifamily properties, which meant that Chicago's NSP2 grant supported larger projects in a smaller number of tracts. NSP2 investment metrics vary within counties as well; Appendix Table 1 shows the distribution of values for each metric by county.

Section 3)   **Empirical strategy and additional data sources**

This paper presents evidence about where grantees targeted their NSP2 investments, what initial housing market conditions prevailed in NSP2 tracts, and how housing markets changed in NSP2 tracts during the program's implementation period, relative to other tracts in the sample counties. We present descriptive statistics on levels and changes for several key housing outcomes: the inventory of distressed properties, vacant properties, volume of arms'-length sales, and (with some limitations) prices of arms'-length sales. Probit models are estimated to explore how pre-NSP2 tract characteristics are correlated with the probability of tracts receiving NSP2 investments. To assess whether tracts that received NSP2 investment experienced the recovery period differently than other tracts in the same county, we estimate reduced-form OLS regressions on housing market changes as a function of NSP2 expenditures, controlling for initial tract characteristics. NSP2 tracts are compared to all non-NSP2 tracts in the same county and two plausibly more appropriate comparison groups: tracts that had previously received other housing subsidy programs and below-median income tracts. Below we discuss the empirical strategy in more approach, as well as challenges to identifying the impact of NSP2 investments.

3.1)   Addressing potential tract selection bias

The primary challenge to assessing whether NSP2 caused changes in neighborhood housing markets is the potential for tract selection bias: NSP2 tracts may differ from non-NSP2 tracts in ways that would have altered their trajectories during the study period even in the absence of the program. The probability of selection bias seems quite high, however, the direction of the bias relative to possible control tracts is not obvious *a priori*. Grantees were required in their applications to target tracts considered at high risk for foreclosure and vacancy, based on a set of "risk scores" developed by HUD.[7] Therefore in the absence of NSP2, we might expect housing outcomes in NSP2 tracts to be worse over the course of the recovery than those in non-NSP2 tracts. However, the program's goal was to concentrate investments in tracts that were capable of improvement, not necessarily "worst case" tracts. Grantees were also

---

[7] Tracts with a foreclosure risk score, or averaged foreclosure and vacancy risk score, of 18 to 20 were eligible for NSP. For geographic continuity, HUD also permitted grantees to include adjacent tracts with lower risk scores as long as the average risk score across all targeted tracts was 18 or above. The methodology used for calculating risk scores is described at http://www.huduser.org/portal/datasets/nsp_foreclosure_data.html.

encouraged to leverage NSP2 funds with other public or philanthropic funds, which may have steered NSP2 towards tracts with particular local assets. In these instances, NSP2 tracts may have had better prospects than some initially distressed tracts that were not targeted for NSP2.

Qualitative interviews conducted with grantees during the evaluation suggested that both types of selection occurred, sometimes in the same county. Some grantees indicated that they targeted tracts where they had prior relationships with non-profit affordable housing organizations, anchor institutions or local foundations. This is consistent with research by Fraser and Oakley (2015) and Reid (2011), who found that grantees often used NSP in neighborhoods with long-standing plans for revitalization. In other cases, grantees faced political pressure to channel NSP2 funds to neighborhoods with long-standing challenges that probably could be not resolved with NSP2 (Abt Associates 2014). Therefore it is difficult to predict the net effect of selection bias, which may also differ across counties.

There are two additional reasons to consider that NSP2 tracts might not have been systematically better or worse than non-NSP2 tracts. First, Reid (2011) points out that geographically specific information on foreclosures and REO properties was not available to HUD or grantees at the time that NSP was first adopted. Therefore HUD used proxy variables, such as the percentage of high-cost loans from HMDA, and county-wide data on housing prices and unemployment rates, to predict tract-level risk of foreclosure and vacancy. These data limitations make it unclear whether high scoring tracts that grantees targeted for NSP really had worse housing conditions at the time of application.

Second, implementation of NSP2 required grantees to acquire individual properties from among the distressed and vacant inventory available at that time, introducing some degree of random selection at the property level. The interviews suggest that grantees faced considerable difficulty acquiring foreclosed properties in their intended neighborhoods, because of limited availability, competition with investors, property physical conditions, and various regulatory and bureaucratic impediments (Abt Associates 2014).[8] Some of these factors (particularly investor competition) may be correlated with tract housing market outcomes, but others (such as banks withholding foreclosures from sale and bureaucratic impediments within the NSP2 program) are potentially orthogonal to outcomes of interest.

A further suggestion of exogenous variation in tract selection is shown by discrepancies in which tracts were targeted in grantee applications and which ones ultimately received NSP2 investment. In Cook County, only 12 percent of the tracts targeted in the initial application received any NSP2 activity. In Los Angeles and Maricopa Counties, slightly more than half of initially targeted census tracts received NSP2 investment. By contrast, Wayne County only targeted 17 census tracts for investment, and ended up working in 75 additional tracts not initially targeted. Some of the discrepancies between targeted and treated tracts could be driven by grantees receiving smaller than requested NSP2 allocations, but interviews with grantees suggested that most of the geographic variation was driven by difficulty in acquiring suitable properties in their targeted neighborhoods within the program deadlines.[9]

We use several approaches to create appropriate comparison groups. First, as described in Section 3.2 below, we estimate probit models to ascertain which observable tract characteristics prior to NSP2 are predictive of NSP2 investment locations. These characteristics are then controlled for in the regressions on housing market change. Second, because we cannot

---

[8] Several grantees mentioned property physical conditions as limiting factors, either because poor quality would require too much work to rehab, or aversions to specific attributes, such as swimming pools.

[9] Some prior studies have used the variation in treatment status among eligible or targeted subjects as the basis for quasi-experimental research design (for instance, evaluations of Moving-to-Opportunity by Ludwig et al (2008) and Katz et al (2001)). In this framework, the eligible or targeted by untargeted subjects form the control group. However, in our seven sample counties, there are not enough NSP2 targeted but untreated tracts to serve as a control group. Nor can we use the HUD risk scores in a regression discontinuity analysis, because eligibility for NSP2 was not set by a strictly observed cutoff score.

directly observe the presence of tract assets, such as anchor institutions or non-profit housing providers, we rely on a proxy indicator to define a comparison group: whether the tract has previously received other housing programs. Specifically, we identify tracts that have housing activities funded through CDBG, HOME, LIHTC or the first round of NSP (NSP1). Tracts previously served by these programs may have similar unobservable characteristics to NSP2 tracts, but because NSP2 was much more limited in scale, many fewer tracts received NSP2 funding.[10] Third, because NSP2 tracts were selected based on distressed or disadvantaged conditions, we construct an alternate comparison group from all non-NSP2 tracts that initially fell below median income for the county. There is some overlap between tracts with other housing programs and low-income tracts; the amount of overlap varies across counties. In the descriptive analysis and regressions shown in Section 4, changes in housing market outcomes for NSP2 tracts are thus compared to all non-NSP2 tracts in the same counties, tracts with other housing programs, and low-income tracts. Because tract selection strategies varied across counties and across grantees within counties, we do not have strong priors on which comparison group provides the best correction for selection bias, and present results for all three potential comparison groups.[11]

3.2)   Empirical strategy

The first part of the analysis explores pre-NSP2 housing market conditions in NSP2 tracts and various comparison groups, and seeks to determine what pre-treatment characteristics are predictive of NSP2 investment location. We present descriptive statistics and graphs on tract characteristics, particularly three housing market outcomes (distressed property inventory,

---

[10] Prior funding through other housing programs is likely to have a direct influence on housing outcomes, so these programs are not appropriate to use as an instrument for NSP2 funding, but can be used to form a comparison group.
[11] We tried similar analysis using propensity score matching to construct comparison groups. Because this method also relies on observable variables for matching, it offers no conceptual advantage to the current method, and regression results are generally consistent with those presented here. Results available upon request from authors.

vacancies, and sales volume). To more formally explore the determinants of NSP2 tract selection, we also estimate probit models on the binary outcome of NSP2 treatment as a function of baseline housing market outcomes (levels and lagged changes), other housing programs, and a variety of population and neighborhood characteristics. The general form of the probit model is shown below in Equation 1.

(1) $\quad \Pr(NSP2_i = 1) = \beta_0 + \beta_1 HSGMKT_i + \beta_2 OTHPOLICY_i + \beta_3 POP_i + PLACE_j + \varepsilon_i$

In the equation, i indexes the census tract, j indexes the census place. *NSP2* is a binary variable that equals one if any NSP2 investment was made in the tract during the 2009-2013 period. *HSGMKT* is a vector of housing market metrics, observed as levels in 2009 and changes from 2006-2009 (roughly the years of the housing collapse). *OTHPOLICY* is a binary indicator of whether the tract had any housing-related projects funded through CDBG, HOME, LIHTC or NSP1, as of 2009.[12] *POP* is a vector of population and neighborhood characteristics prior to NSP2 (most are taken from the 2005-2009 ACS). *PLACE* is a set of fixed effects for census place (city, town or CDP), and ε is an error term. Regressions are estimated separately for each of the seven sample counties, to allow for varying tract selection strategies. Standard errors are clustered by PUMA to adjust for possible spatial correlation among adjacent census tracts.[13] More details on variable definition and data sources is provided in Section 3.4 below and in Table 4. Summary statistics on all variables for NSP2 tracts, by county, are shown in Table 5; Appendix Table 2 shows summary statistics for the variables, combining all tracts and counties.

The sample is limited to census places in which at least one census tract received NSP2 investment or was targeted for investment in a grantee's application. This restriction is imposed

---

[12] Alternate specifications using the number of housing projects or expenditures on projects yield substantively similar results.
[13] Public Use Microdata Areas (PUMAs) are clusters of geographically contiguous census tracts with total population of roughly 100,000. They are often used as proxies for housing and labor submarkets within large metropolitan areas.

because many of the grantees are local government agencies that can only work within their political jurisdiction, and helps to control for unobserved factors that may vary across political boundaries within a single county (for instance, school quality or crime prevention provided by city governments). Six of the seven counties have NSP2 activity in multiple cities within the county; the exception is Philadelphia, in which the city and county are co-terminus.

The second part of the analysis examines changes in three housing market outcomes – distress, vacancies and sales volume – from 2009 and 2013. These years bookend the implementation period for NSP2, and correspond roughly to the national economic recovery (NBER identifies June 2009 as the trough of the recession). We present graphic evidence of changes for NSP2 tracts, tracts with other housing policies, low-income tracts, and all non-NSP2 tracts. All changes are calculated according to the following formula:

(2) $$dDistress = \frac{Distress_{2013} - Distress_{2009}}{0.5*(Distress_{2009} + Distress_{2013})}$$

Unlike a standard percentage change, this change measure provides a symmetric growth rate, particularly for large value changes, that is a better fit with OLS estimation (see Davis et al 1996, Haltiwanger et al 2010). The change metric takes on values from -2 to 2.

Besides the graphical analysis of housing market changes, we estimate reduced-form OLS regressions of housing changes as a function of NSP2 investment. The general form is shown in Equation 3 below:

(3) $$dDistress_{it,t+1} = \beta_0 + \beta_1 NSP2_i + \beta_2 X_{it} + PLACE_j + \varepsilon_{it}$$

In the equation, i indexes the census tract, j indexes the census place, and t indexes the time period. *dDistress* is the change from 2009 to 2013 in the inventory of distressed properties; other dependent variables used are change in vacancies and change in sales volume. The key independent variable is *NSP2*, an indicator of NSP2 treatment per census tract. X is a vector of

16

baseline housing market conditions, other housing programs, population and neighborhood characteristics. All models include fixed effects for census place, and have standard errors clustered by PUMA. As with the tract selection analysis, the sample is limited to census places with NSP2 investment activity or targeted for NSP2.

3.3)   Measuring NSP2 treatment

We use two different metrics of NSP2 investment: a binary indicator for any NSP2 activity in a tract, and the total NSP2 expenditures divided by tract median housing value. As shown in Tables 3 and 4, there is substantial variation across counties and tracts in the type of NSP2 activity, the number of properties, and amount of funds expended. Such details of NSP2 investment could plausibly affect the impact of NSP2 on tract housing outcomes. For instance, it is likely that a tract where NSP2 was primarily used to demolish blighted structures, resulting in a smaller housing stock but increased prevalence of empty lots, may have different housing outcomes than a tract where NSP2 was invested in rehabilitation or redevelopment. Five of the seven counties essentially specialized in a single activity – rehab for the Sand State counties, demolition/land-banking for Cuyahoga and Wayne – so estimating regressions separately by county simplifies the measurement of activity type. Unfortunately in the two counties that pursued mixed strategies (Cook and Philadelphia), the number of tracts using each activity is too small to estimate separate impacts.

It is also plausible that larger investments – by expenditure levels, number of properties, or property size – will have greater impact on surrounding housing markets. Expenditures are the preferred metric of investment size, because it should reflect a number of other features, including number of properties, property size, and potentially quality of rehab work (i.e. material cost) for which we have limited direct measurement (notably, unit counts or other property size measures). Because property values and therefore purchase prices may be higher in less distressed tracts, expenditures are divided by tract median housing values, to better reflect the relative size of NSP2 investments. Regressions were also estimated using dummy variables for "high concentration" NSP2 tracts, based on the number of treated properties. Results were generally consistent with those using normalized expenditures (available from authors upon request).

We estimate changes in housing outcomes over the full implementation period as a function of total spending during this time, rather than annual or other incremental changes and spending, for several reasons. The majority of NSP2 properties were completed within the last several months before the February 2013 expenditure deadline (indeed some had not been completed when the grantees provided final data), so there would be little observed annual activity in the early years of the program. We are also agnostic about when during the activity period spillovers would be apparent (particularly for longer rehab projects). And as a practical limitation, our data do not allow us to observe expenditure levels for intermediate time periods.

A final caveat on measuring NSP2 investment is that there may be more heterogeneity in "treatment" than we are able to capture using expenditures. More nuanced characteristics of treated properties – such as age and aesthetic appeal of structures, physical condition, quality of rehab work, and visual appearance during the investment period – are likely to be heterogeneous across treated tracts. Data on these characteristics are not available, so they cannot be included in regressions, but this is an area that could benefit from qualitative case studies of individual NSP2 projects.

3.4)   Additional data sources

In addition to the NSP2 property-level data, the analysis uses secondary data from a number of sources. All variables are measured using constant 2000 tract boundaries. Variable definitions are shown in Table 4; summary statistics for NSP2 tracts by county are shown in Table 5 and for all tracts combined in Appendix Table 2.

Information on financially distressed residential properties and housing transactions from 2006 through the first quarter of 2013 were purchased from Core Logic. An inventory of distressed properties is created by aggregating all properties in any stage of distress: any property after filing of a foreclosure start or sale and prior to exit from REO is flagged as in distress. When shown in levels, distress is expressed as a ratio per 1000 total housing units; changes over time are based on counts of distress (because the denominator does not change).[14] Sales volume is measured as the number of arms'-length transactions per tract-year, for one- to four-family properties and condominiums. Transaction data is also used to calculate the share of sales purchased by non-owner-occupants (investors). More details on cleaning and variable construction using the Core Logic data is available in the technical appendix of the HUD report (Abt Associates 2014).

To identify which tracts received non-NSP2 housing programs, property-level data was obtained from HUD on four housing subsidy programs: CDBG, HOME (excluding single-family), LIHTC and NSP1. Project geocoded locations and completion dates were used to flag tracts with at least one housing project completed prior to 2009. Vacancy data obtained from the U.S. Postal Service is used to calculate vacant housing units per 1000 total housing units.

---

[14] Housing stock in the NSP tracts and control tracts in the sample counties are predominately single-family structures, so using total housing units as the denominator is a reasonable approximation for properties that have outstanding mortgages. Robustness checks using distressed properties per housing units in one- to four-family structures yield similar results.

Variables on population and neighborhood characteristics, such as population density, median household income, race and ethnicity, and housing stock composition, are taken from the 2005-2009 American Community Survey.

One standard housing market metric, sales prices, is problematic because of the time frame under study. During the recession and recovery, the volume of arms' length sales was quite thin, so constructing annual price measures for small geographic areas such as census tracts is difficult. Restricting the sample to tracts with at least 10 arms' length sales per year in both 2009 and 2012 eliminates approximately 20 percent of NSP2 treated tracts and tracts in comparison groups, with higher shares for Cook, Cuyahoga and Wayne Counties. Moreover, this introduces selection bias, because tracts with higher sales volume have higher average prices. It is also likely that individual properties that went on the market during this time period differ in value from average properties in the tract that did not transact. Therefore we present graphs of housing price levels and change for illustrative purposes, but do not use prices in the main regression analyses. Regressions on price changes are presented in Appendix Table 5, and present generally similar results to the other dependent variables, but cannot be estimated for Cook County or using the two comparison groups. Caution should be used in interpreting all of the price results.

Section 4)   Results

As intended by the legislation, NSP2 grantees targeted neighborhoods that had substantial inventories of distressed and/or vacant properties prior to the program. Most NSP2 tracts had below median income residents, large black and Hispanic population shares, and had previously received investments from other housing programs. During NSP2 implementation, the inventory of distressed properties in NSP2 tracts fell substantially in all sample counties. Changes in vacancies and sales volume in NSP2 tracts varied more across counties. There are few statistically significant differences in housing market changes between NSP2 tracts and other tracts in the same counties.

4.1) Descriptive statistics: Housing market conditions in NSP2 tracts

Although the impetus for NSP2 emerged from the foreclosure crisis, the program was designed to address both the current problem of financially distressed properties (those in foreclosure or REO) and long-standing vacant or abandoned properties. Grantees in four sample counties – Cook, Cuyahoga, Philadelphia and Wayne - used NSP2 in tracts where vacancy rates substantially exceeded distress rates (Table 5). NSP2 tracts in Los Angeles had substantially higher distress rates than vacancy rates, while Maricopa and Miami used NSP2 in tracts with roughly similar rates of financial distress and vacancy. Average rates of financial distress in NSP2 tracts varied from 18 properties per 1000 housing units in Philadelphia) to 130 per 1000 in Maricopa. Vacancy rates ranged from 30 per 1000 houses in Los Angeles, to 226 per 1000 in Wayne. The difference in type and extent of housing market weakness influenced the different choice of strategies used by NSP2 grantees across counties.

Two other metrics in Table 5 illustrate the weakness of housing markets in NSP2 tracts at the beginning of the program. With the exception of Los Angeles and Maricopa, the annual volume of arms'-length housing sales (excluding properties sold during foreclosure) was quite thin – around 30 per tract in Miami, Philadelphia and Wayne, fewer than twenty per tract-year in Cook and Cuyahoga. The thinness of sales activity likely introduces selection bias in observed sales prices; homeowners who are not in immediate economic distress will likely choose not to sell their property in such a weak market. Consistent with this hypothesis, median prices from arms'-length sales reported by Core Logic are much lower than self-reported housing values from the ACS, except in Philadelphia (although since the tract-level ACS data is only reported for five-year rolling averages, this discrepancy may also reflect the fall in housing prices over the 2005-2009 period).

Grantees targeted NSP2 investments to tracts that had previously received other housing programs (middle section of Table 5). About half the NSP2 tracts in Los Angeles had at least one other housing program, while nearly all the NSP2 tracts in Cuyahoga and Wayne had prior housing programs. These numbers corroborate statements in grantee interviews that they tried to use NSP2 in neighborhoods where they had made prior investments and had existing relationships. Not surprisingly, most NSP2 tracts fell in the bottom half of the income distribution for their respective counties, although in Los Angeles and Philadelphia approximately one-third of NSP2 tracts were above median income. Most NSP2 tracts were majority black or Hispanic populations. Except in Philadelphia, the housing stock in NSP2 neighborhoods was primarily one- to four-family properties; these properties tended to have higher rates of foreclosure than multifamily buildings.

Table 5 shows a static picture of NSP2 tracts at the beginning of the program. Figures 1-6 illustrate how housing conditions in NSP2 tracts changed during the crisis (2006-2009) and recovery periods (2009-2013). The graphs show average changes for NSP2 tracts, the two comparison groups – tracts with other housing programs and below-median income tracts – as well as for all non-NSP2 tracts.

The inventory of distressed properties grew substantially during the 2006-2009 period in nearly all tract groups and counties, particularly in the Sand State counties of Los Angeles, Maricopa and Miami (Figure 1). Distressed property changes in NSP2 tracts were not significantly different than in any of the comparison groups in Cook and Maricopa Counties. In Cuyahoga, Miami-Dade, Philadelphia and Wayne Counties, distressed properties in NSP2 tracts increased by less than in at least one of the comparison groups. In Los Angeles County, NSP2 properties saw larger increases in distressed properties than all non-NSP2 tracts. The rapid growth in distressed property inventory caused by the foreclosure crisis improved substantially during the recovery period of 2009-2013, which also coincides with NSP2 implementation (Figure 2). Distressed property inventories dropped by significantly more in NSP2 tracts than in at least one comparison group in Los Angeles, Maricopa, and Wayne Counties. In the other four counties, decreases in distressed properties among NSP2 tracts were not statistically different than in any of the three comparison groups.

Vacancy changes during the housing crisis and recovery are much more varied across counties, but also somewhat consistent across tract groups within counties (Figures 3-4). Two of the counties with high levels of vacancies in 2009 –Cuyahoga and Philadelphia – did not see growth in vacancies during the housing crisis, suggesting that their vacant properties were a longer run problem (Figure 3). Wayne County saw increased vacancies during the crisis, contributing to its high level in 2009. The largest growth in vacancies 2006-2009 came in the three Sand State counties. In Cook, Los Angeles and Maricopa Counties, vacancies rose more in NSP2 tracts than in at least of the non-NSP2 comparison groups. For nearly all counties, the direction of change in vacancies flipped during the recovery period (Figure 4). Cook, Los Angeles, Maricopa and Miami saw decreased vacancies in all tract groups from 2009-2013, with largest drops in Maricopa. Cuyahoga and Wayne saw increased vacancies, while in Philadelphia changes varied across tract groups. In Cuyahoga, vacancies increased by significantly less in NSP2 tracts than two of the comparison groups, and in Los Angeles, NSP2 tracts had significantly larger drops in vacancy than all three comparison groups. In Wayne County, NSP2 tracts saw larger growth in vacancies than two of the comparison groups. Among the other counties, vacancy changes were not statistically different across NSP2 and comparison tracts.

All tract groups in all counties saw substantial drops in the number of housing sales during the crisis years, with largest decreases in Miami and the smallest in Los Angeles and Maricopa (Figure 5). In Los Angeles and Maricopa, NSP2 tracts had smaller drops in sales volume than at least two of the comparison groups. In Miami-Dade and Philadelphia, sales volume in NSP2 tracts was significantly larger than in all non-NSP2 tracts. The 2009-2013 period saw uneven recovery in sales volume across counties (Figure 6). Los Angeles, Miami and Wayne Counties saw the strongest recovery in sales volume. Sales volume dropped by the largest amount in Cuyahoga. In Los Angeles and Maricopa, sales volume changes in NSP2 tracts significantly lagged at least two comparison groups. In Cuyahoga, sales dropped by significantly less in NSP2 tracts than in other low-income tracts.

4.2) What neighborhood characteristics predict location of NSP2 investment?

As suggested by the descriptive statistics, there is some cross-county variation in how grantees targeted NSP2 investments, but some neighborhood characteristics consistently predict NSP2 tract selection across counties (Table 6).

In particular, counties vary in whether they targeted NSP2 towards tracts with financially distressed properties or high vacancy rates. Distress rates are positively correlated with NSP2 tract selection in Los Angeles and Philadelphia, but negatively correlated in Cook, Cuyahoga and Maricopa. By contrast, vacancy rates positively predict NSP2 tract selection in Cook and Maricopa. Grantees in three counties – Cook, Los Angeles and Maricopa – were more likely to use NSP2 in tracts with high sales volume. In Cuyahoga – which primarily used NSP2 for land-banking - sales volume was negatively correlated with NSP2 tract selection. The regressions also include controls for changes in distress, vacancy and sales volume during the 2006-2009 period, although these variables are not consistently predictive of NSP2 location.

Also consistent with descriptive statistics in Table 5, grantees were more likely to place their NSP2 investments in tracts that previously received other housing programs. The coefficient on other programs is positive and strongly significant in four counties (Cuyahoga, Maricopa, Miami and Wayne), positive and weakly significant in Cook and Los Angeles, and positive although not statistically significant in Philadelphia.

Tract relative income status does not appear to have determined NSP2 tract selection in five of the seven counties. Low income status is positively predictive of NSP2 location in Maricopa, but negatively predictive in Los Angeles. Because NSP2 funds were quite limited, in all counties, there were many low-income tracts that did not receive any NSP2 investments. However, including median household income in the regressions as a continuous variable also does not yield significant results. On the other hand, black and/or Latino population shares are positive and at least weakly significant predictors of NSP2 tract selection in six of the seven counties. In Wayne County, the estimated coefficients on both black and Latino population shares are negative and significant, although NSP2 tracts in Wayne were on average 80 percent black, the highest share across all seven counties.

4.3)   How did housing markets change in NSP2 tracts during recovery?

Regression analysis on housing market changes from 2009-2013 is conducted using three different outcome variables: financially distressed properties (Table 7), vacancies (Table 8), and arms' length sales (Table 9). Each table presents results by county, for four specifications. In the first column, NSP2 presence is measured as a binary indicator. Regressions in columns 2-4 use the natural log of NSP2 expenditures divided by tract median housing value. The set of tracts also varies across specifications: regressions in columns 1-2 include all non-NSP2 tracts as the comparison group, column 3 includes only tracts with other housing programs, and column 4 includes only below-median income tracts.

Beginning with changes in distressed properties, there is essentially no evidence that NSP2 tracts experienced different trajectories than non-NSP2 tracts, or that the amount of NSP2 spending is correlated with changes in distress (Table 7). The coefficient on NSP2 activity is statistically significant only in two of the 28 regressions presented: Column 1 for Cuyahoga and Column 3 for Maricopa. Both are positive, indicating that NSP2 activity is associated with smaller decreases in distress (on average, all tracts saw decreases in distress). But the lack of consistently significant results either for those counties across other specifications, or across counties for the same specification, makes it difficult to infer a robust association. In general, the signs and estimated magnitudes on NSP2 activity are fairly consistent within counties across specifications, even using different samples in columns 3 and 4.

The analysis of vacancies provides more evidence that NSP2 tracts in Cook and Cuyahoga counties saw different changes in vacancies during the recovery period (Table 8). For Cook County, the coefficient on NSP2 activity is positive in all specifications and significant in three. On average tracts in Cook saw drops in vacancies, so these results suggest that NSP2 presence or spending is associated with smaller decreases in vacancies, conditional on baseline characteristics. That is, NSP2 tracts did not improve as much as non-NSP2 tracts. In Cuyahoga, which on average saw increased vacancies during the 2009-2013 period, the negative and significant coefficients suggest that NSP2 activity was associated with smaller increases in vacancy – a potentially beneficial effect of NSP2. Among the other five counties, none of the estimated coefficients are significant at the five percent level, but once again signs and magnitudes are quite consistent within counties across specifications.

There is some evidence that NSP2 tracts in Cuyahoga and Los Angeles Counties saw stronger recovery in sales volume (Table 9). In Cuyahoga, the coefficients on NSP2 activity are positive and significant in all four specifications. From Figure 6, Cuyahoga tracts on average saw continued drops in sales volume during 2009-2013, so these results suggest that NSP2 tracts fell by less. In Los Angeles, all four coefficients on NSP2 activity are positive, two are significant at the five percent level and one at the ten percent level. On average, tracts in Los Angeles saw a small increase in sales volume during the recovery. While NSP2 tracts on average had decreased sales, the regression results suggest that, conditional on observable neighborhood characteristics, NSP2 activity was positively correlated with sales volume. There is somewhat less robust evidence in Table 9 that NSP2 activity in Miami was associated with smaller increases in sales volume; the coefficient on NSP2 spending is at least marginally significant in two specifications.

Considering the results from all three housing market outcomes, Cuyahoga shows the most robust evidence that NSP2 activity is correlated with a stronger housing recovery, namely smaller increases in vacancy and smaller decreases in sales volume. Cook and Los Angeles Counties show consistent relationships between NSP2 activity and one housing market outcome each, although in Cook the results suggest weaker recovery in NSP2 tracts. Most of the counties do not show evidence that NSP2 tracts had differential changes in housing markets during the recovery period. The results presented here are robust to a variety of other specifications using different combinations of control variables and functional forms of those variables, including different measurement of NSP2 activity.

Section 5)   Conclusion

The federal Neighborhood Stabilization Program was intended to provide support to cities and neighborhoods that were particularly hard-hit by foreclosed and vacant properties. The program was designed to allow grantees flexibility, so that they could tailor their strategies to fit local housing conditions and build on institutional strengths and expertise. While the funds allocated for NSP were small relative to the overall housing stock and the scale of the foreclosure crisis, for many localities the amount of funding was comparable to or greater than funds received through CDBG or other affordable housing programs.

Grantees' approach to NSP2, characterized by the type of activity and targeted locations, varied across counties. In Cuyahoga and Wayne Counties, with high vacancy rates resulting from long-term population decline, grantees chose to spend NSP2 on demolition and land-banking. By contrast, grantees in Los Angeles, Maricopa and Miami-Dade primarily focused on rehab and redevelopment, while Cook and Philadelphia pursued mixed strategies. The number of properties completed and cost per property also varied across grantees and counties. The median NSP2 tract received about three properties and $400,000 dollars – quite small compared to the housing stock and scale of distress. The selection of NSP2 tracts is correlated with initial housing market characteristics – such as the frequency of distressed and/or vacant properties – as well as demographic characteristics. Tracts that had previously received other housing subsidies were more likely to be selected for NSP2 investments.

The evidence of housing recovery during the NSP2 implementation period is quite mixed. NSP2 tracts in all counties saw substantial decreases in the inventory of distressed properties, as fewer properties entered foreclosure and the stock of REO properties was reduced. Changes in vacancy rates and sales volume varied across counties. There is some evidence that

NSP2 activity in Cuyahoga County is correlated with stronger recovery, measured by smaller increases in vacancy and smaller decreases in sales volume. Results also suggest that NSP2 activity in Cook County was positively correlated with vacancy changes, and NSP2 spending in Los Angeles was positively correlated with growth in sales volume. In other counties, there is not consistent evidence that NSP2 activity is associated with differential housing recovery.

A plausible reason for the lack of consistent results is the small scale of NSP2 activity in most targeted tracts. But some data limitations may also hinder our ability to precisely measure the program's impact. We do not have direct information on some tract-level assets or liabilities that could be correlated with NSP2 activity and with housing market changes, such as where local governments and non-profits used non-NSP2 funds for housing development or foreclosure mitigation efforts. Rather, we rely on observation of other housing programs to infer other activity, but this may be a noisy or biased measure. We also have limited data on changes in private capital's role in tract housing markets over time. It is also possible that the heterogeneous approach of grantees to implementing NSP2 within counties is not well captured by the relative expenditure metric we use.

Finally, it is possible that it is simply too early to detect the impacts of NSP2. The changes are measured through early 2013, roughly simultaneous with the expenditure deadline. Many individual properties were not completed until nearly that time, so perhaps any spillovers to tracts had not yet been captured. On the other hand, the purpose of stimulus programs is to speed up the pace of recovery. If NSP did not generate tangible impacts until the end of its three-year implementation period, it may cast doubt on whether housing rehab and demolition are effective stimulus tools.

References

Abt Associates. Jan. 2003. Exploring the Impacts of the HOPE IV Program on Surrounding Neighborhoods. Report submitted to Office of Public Housing Investments and U.S. Department of Housing and Urban Development.

Abt Associates Inc. 2014. Evaluation of the Neighborhood Stabilization Program (NSP2). Washington DC: U.S. Department of Housing and Urban Development Final Report.

Baum-Snow, Nathaniel and Justin Marion. 2009. The Effects of Low Income Housing Tax Credit Developments on Neighborhoods. Journal of Public Economics, 93(5): 654-666.

Been, V., S. Chan, I. Ellen, and J. Madar. 2011. Decoding the Foreclosure Crisis: Causes, Responses, and Consequences. Journal of Policy Analysis and Management 30 (2): 388–396.

Campbell, J. Y., S. Giglio, and P. Pathak. 2011. Forced Sales and House Prices. American Economic Review 101 (5): 2108–31.

Davis, Peter. 1996. Spatial competition in retail markets: movie theaters. The RAND Journal of Economics 37(4): 964-982.

Di, Wenhua, Jielai Ma and James Murdoch. 2010. An analysis of the neighborhood impacts of a mortgage assistance program: A spatial hedonic model. Journal of Policy Analysis and Management 29(4): 682-697.

ElBoghdady, Dina. 2007. Housing Crisis Knocks Loudly in Michigan. Washington Post.

Ellen, Ingrid Gould, Johanna Lacoe, and Claudia Ayanna Sharygin. 2013. Do Foreclosures Cause Crime? Journal of Urban Economics 74: 59-70.

Ellen, I.G., A.E. Schwartz, I. Voicu and M.H. Schill. 2007. Does Federally Subsidized Rental Housing Depress Neighborhood Property Values? Journal of Policy Analysis and Management, 26(2): 257-280.

Ellen, Ingrid Gould and Ioan Voicu. 2006. Nonprofit Housing and Neighborhood Spillovers. Journal of Policy Analysis and Management, 25(1): 31-52.

Ergungor, O. Emre and Lisa Nelson. 2012. The Impact of Recovery Efforts on Residential Vacancies. Federal Reserve Bank of Cleveland Working Paper 12-03.

Fraser, James C. and Deirdre Oakley. 2015. The Neighborhood Stabilization Program: Stable for Whom? Journal of Urban Affairs 37(1): 38-41.

Galster, George, Christopher Walker, Christopher Hayes, Patrick Boxall, and Jennifer Johnson. 2004. Measuring the Impact of Community Development Block Grant Spending on Urban Neighborhoods. Housing Policy Debate 15(4): 903-934.

Gerardi, Kristopher, Stephen L. Ross and Paul Willen. 2011. Understanding the Foreclosure Crisis. Journal of Policy Analysis and Management 30(2): 382-388.

Gerardi, K., L. Lambie-Hanson, and P. S. Willen. 2012. Do Borrower Rights Improve Borrower Outcomes? Evidence From the Foreclosure Process. NBER Working Paper Series No. 1766.

Graves, E.M. and E. Shuey. 2013. The Social Impact of Home Rehabilitation in Low-Income Neighborhoods. Federal Reserve Bank of Boston, Community Development Discussion Paper 2013-01.

Griswold, Nigel G., Benjamin Calnin, Michael Schramm, Luc Anselin, and Paul Boehnlein. 2014. Estimating the Effect of Demolishing Distressed Structures in Cleveland, OH, 2009-2013: Impacts on Real Estate Equity and Mortgage-Foreclosure. Report by the Thriving Communities Institute submitted to the Cleveland City Council and Attorney General of Ohio.

Haltiwanger, John, Ron Jarmin and C.J. Krizan. 2010. Mom-and-Pop Meet Big Box: Complements or Substitutes? Journal of Urban Economics 67(1): 116-134.

Hartley, D. 2010. The Effect of Foreclosures on Nearby Housing Prices: Supply or Disamenity? Working paper, Federal Reserve Bank of Cleveland.

Immergluck, Dan. 2012. Too Little, Too Late, and Too Timid: The Federal Response to the Foreclosure Crisis at the Five-Year Mark. Housing Policy Debate.

Immergluck, Dan, and Geoff Smith. 2006. The External Costs of Foreclosure: The Impact of Single-Family Mortgage Foreclosures on Property Values. Housing Policy Debate 17 (1): 57-79.

Jacobs, Jane. 1961. Death and Life of Great American Cities. New York: Random House.

Joice, Paul A. 2011. Neighborhood Stabilization Program. Cityscape 13 (1): 135.

Katz, Lawrence, Jeffrey Kling and Jeffrey Liebman. 2001. Moving to Opportunity in Boston: Early results of a randomized mobility experiment. Quarterly Journal of Economics 116(2): 607-654.

Kotlowitz, Alex. 2009. All Boarded Up. New York Times.

Ludwig, Jens, Jeffrey Liebman, Jeffrey Kling, Greg Duncan, Lawrence Katz, Ronald Kessler, and Lisa Sanbonmatsu. 2008. What Can We Learn About Neighborhood Effects From the Moving to Opportunity Experiment? American Journal of Sociology 114(1): 144-188.

Lin, Z., E. Rosenblatt, and V. W. Yao. 2009. Spillover Effects of Foreclosures on Neighborhood Property Values. The Journal of Real Estate Finance and Economics 38 (4): 387–407.

Mian, A., A. Sufi, and F. Trebbi. 2011. Foreclosures, House Prices, and the Real Economy NBER Working Paper.

Newburger, Harriet. Acquiring Privately Held REO Properties with Public Funds: The case of the Neighborhood Stabilization Program. In REO and Vacant Properties: Strategies for Neighborhood Stabilization. Federal Reserve Banks of Boston and Cleveland and the Federal Reserve Board.

Nickerson, Craig. Acquiring Property for Neighborhood Stabilization: Lessons learned from the front lines. In REO and Vacant Properties: Strategies for Neighborhood Stabilization. Federal Reserve Banks of Boston and Cleveland and the Federal Reserve Board.

Pooley, Karen Beck. 2014. Using Community Development Block Grant Dollars to Revitalize Neighborhoods: The Impact of Program Spending in Philadelphia. Housing Policy Debate, 24(1): 172-191.

Reid, Carolina. 2011. The Neighborhood Stabilization Program: Strategically Targeting Public Investments. Community Investments 23(1): 23-33.

Roth, Alex. 2008. After the Bubble, Ghost Towns Across America. Wall Street Journal.

Schuetz, Jenny, Vicki Been, and Ingrid Gould Ellen. 2008. Neighborhood Effects of Concentrated Mortgage Foreclosures. Journal of Housing Economics 17 (4) (12): 306-19.

Schuetz, Jenny, Jonathan Spader, Jennifer Lewis Buell, Kimberly Burnett, Larry Buron, Alvaro Cortes, Michael DiDomenico, Anna Jefferson, Christian Redfearn and Stephen Whitlow. 2015. Which Way to Recovery? Housing Market Outcomes and the Neighborhood Stabilization Program. Finance and Economics Discussion Series 2015-004, Board of Governors of the Federal Reserve System.

Schwartz, A.E., Ellen, I.G., Voicu, I. and Schill, M.H. 2006. The external effects of place-based subsidized housing. Regional Science and Urban Economics, 36: 679-707.

Shapiro, Samantha. 2008. The Boomtown Mirage. New York Times.

Smith, Marvin M. and Christy Chung Hevener. 2011. The Impact of Housing Rehabilitation on Local Neighborhoods: The Case of Small Community Development Organizations. The American Journal of Economics and Sociology, 70(1): 50-85.

Teaford, Jon. 2010. Urban Renewal and Its Aftermath. Housing Policy Debate 11(2): 443-465.

Whitaker, S., and T. J. Fitzpatrick IV. 2013. Deconstructing Distressed-Property Spillovers: The Effects of Vacant, Tax-Delinquent, and Foreclosed Properties in Housing Submarkets. Journal of Housing Economics 22 (2): 79-91.

Wilson, J.Q. 1963. Planning and Politics: Citizen Participation in Urban Renewal. Journal of the American Institute of Planners 29(4): 242-249.

Zielenbach, Sean and Richard Voith. 2010. HOPE IV and Neighborhood Economic Development: The Importance of Local Market Dynamics. Cityscape 12(1): 99-131.

Figure 1

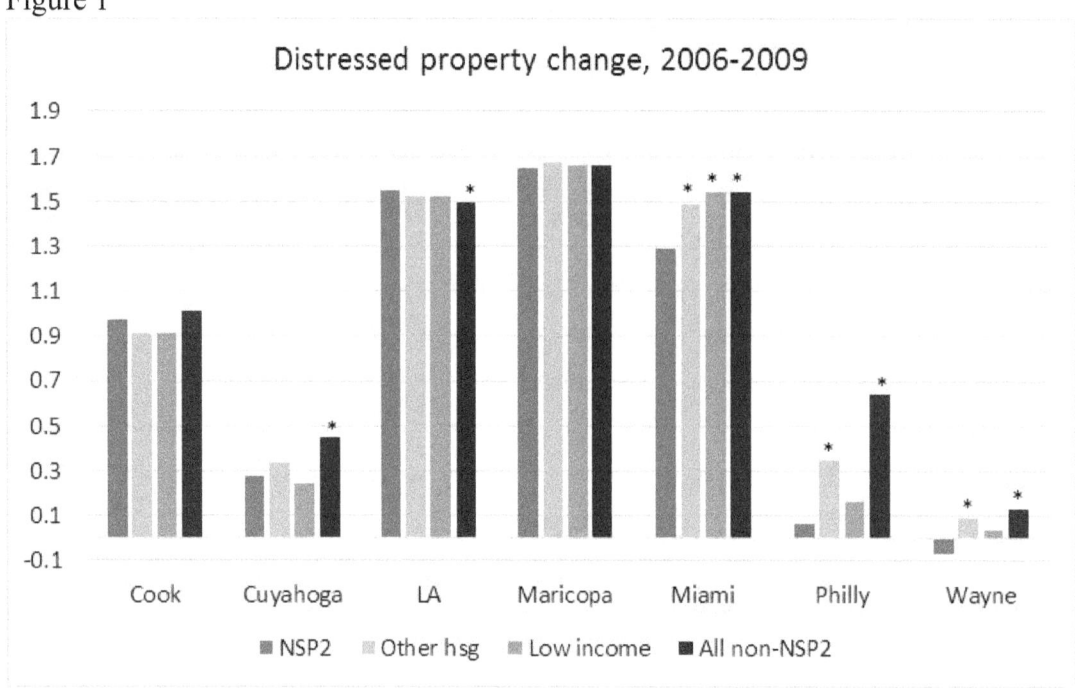

Figure 2:

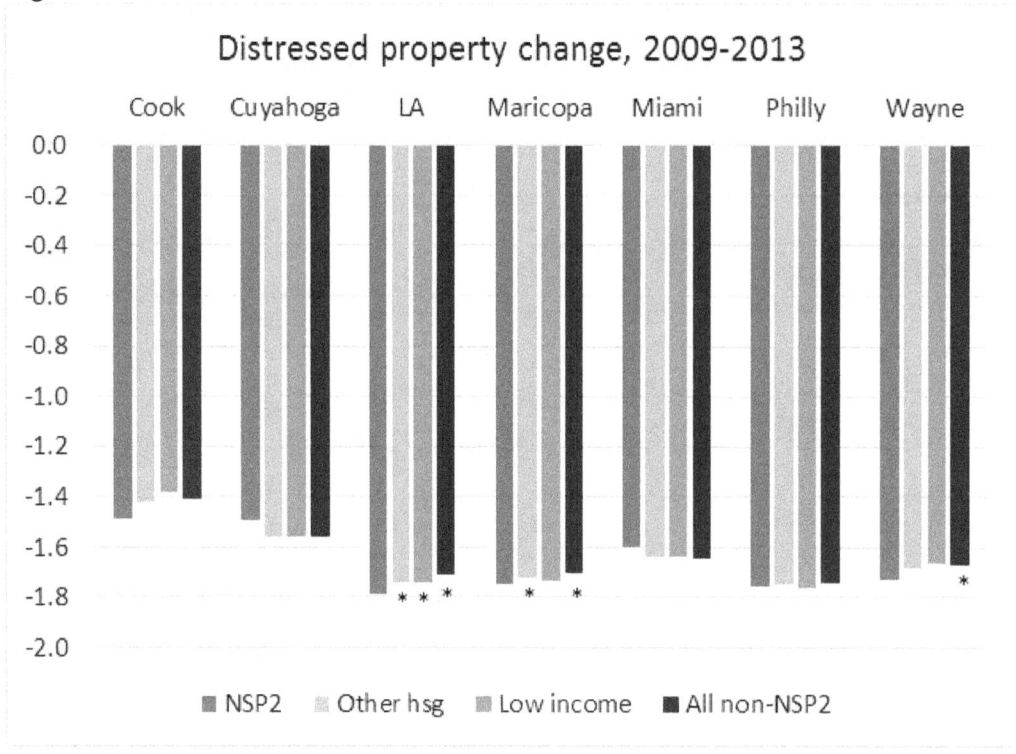

Notes: Figures 1-2 show change rate for properties per tract in any stage of foreclosure or REO. "Other hsg" tracts had properties previously funded by CDBG, HOME, LIHTC or NSP1. "Low income" tracts had median household income below county median income. The three comparison groups are not mutually exclusive. Difference in mean values was calculated between NSP2 tracts and each of the three comparison groups. * $p < 0.05$

Figure 3:

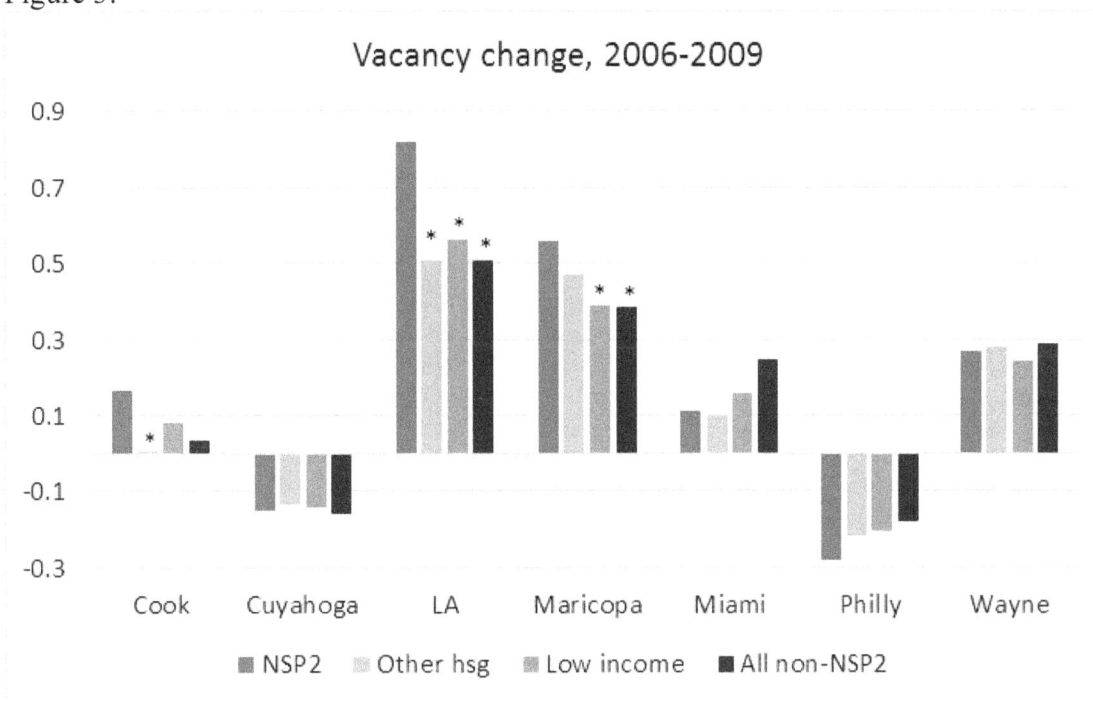

Figure 4

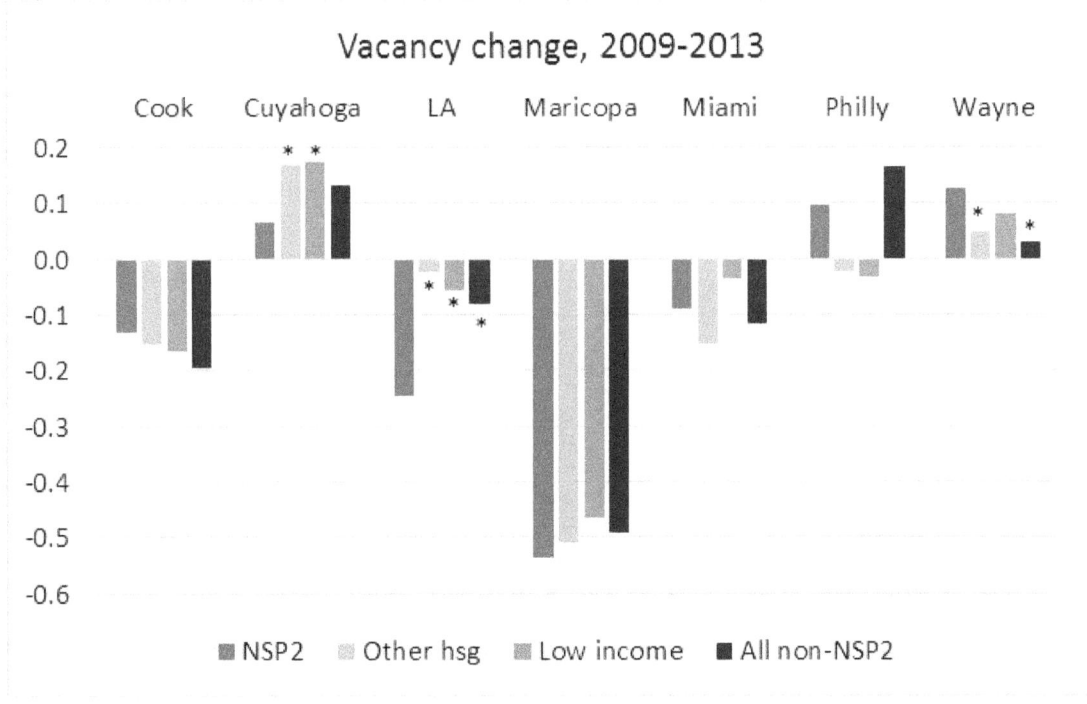

Notes: Figures 3 and 4 show change rate for vacant properties per tract. "Other hsg" tracts had properties previously funded by CDBG, HOME, LIHTC or NSP1. "Low income" tracts had median household income below county median income. The three comparison groups are not mutually exclusive. Difference in mean values was calculated between NSP2 tracts and each of the three comparison groups.
* $p < 0.05$

Figure 5

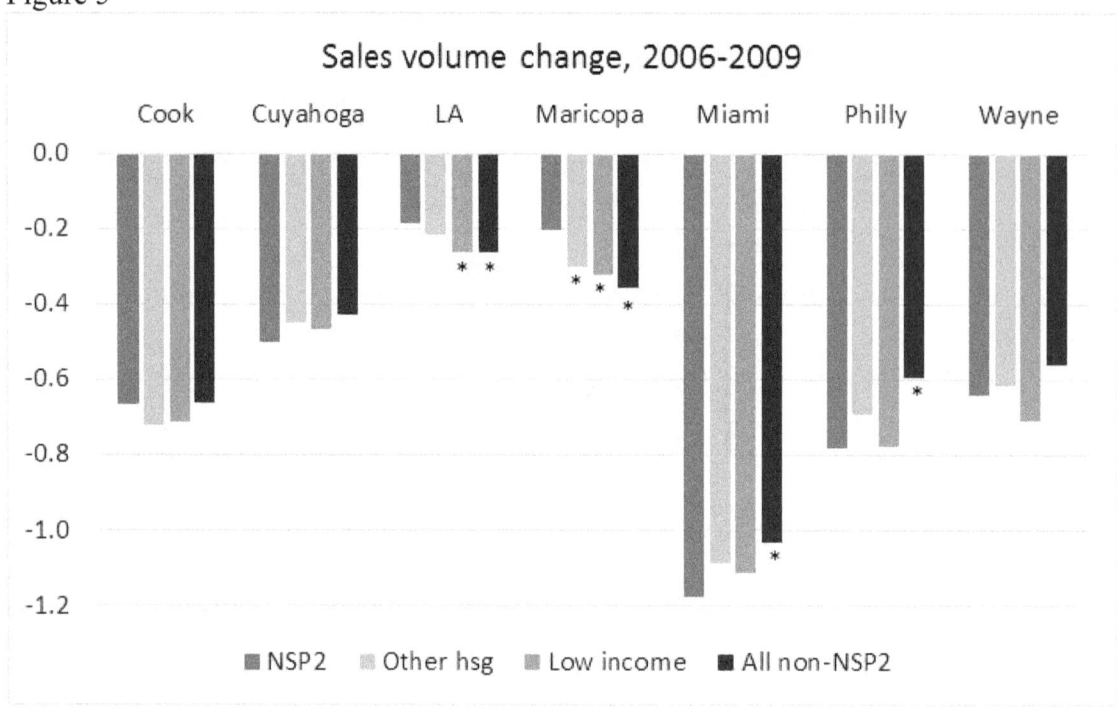

Sales volume change, 2006-2009

Notes: Figures 5 and 6 show change rate for annual arms' length sales per tract. "Other hsg" tracts had properties previously funded by CDBG, HOME, LIHTC or NSP1. "Low income" tracts had median household income below county median income. The three comparison groups are not mutually exclusive. Difference in mean values was calculated between NSP2 tracts and each of the three comparison groups. * $p < 0.05$

Figure 6

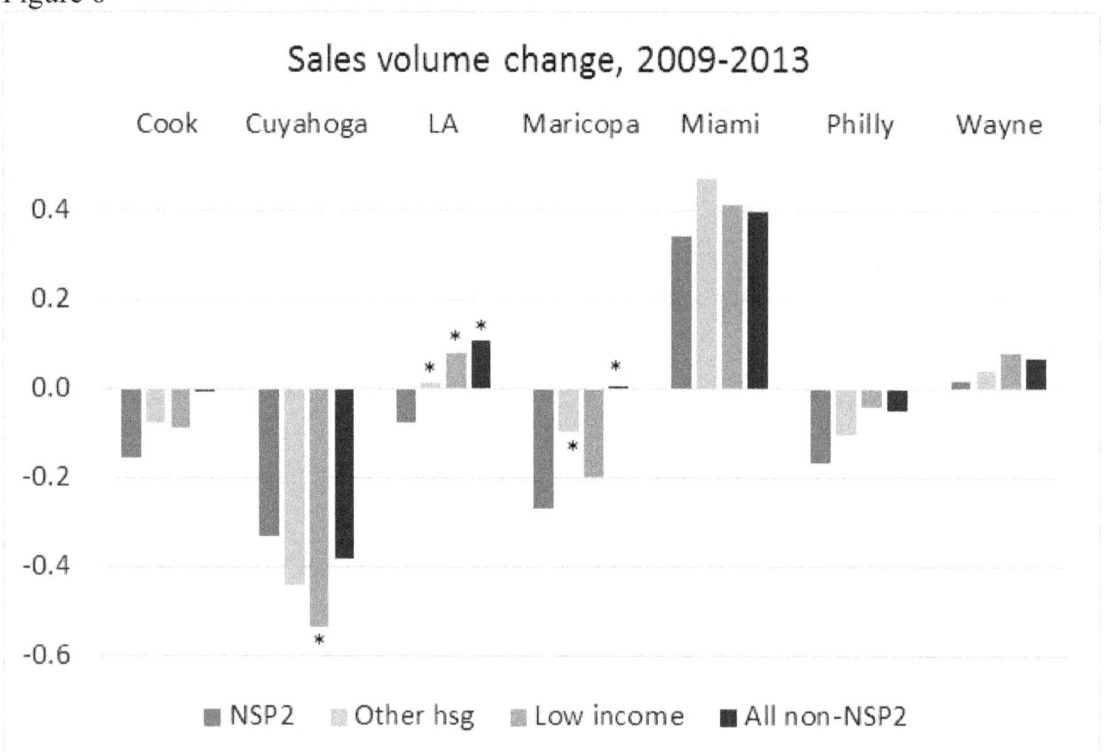

Sales volume change, 2009-2013

Notes: Figures 5 and 6 show change rate for annual arms' length sales per tract. "Other hsg" tracts had properties previously funded by CDBG, HOME, LIHTC or NSP1. "Low income" tracts had median household income below county median income. The three comparison groups are not mutually exclusive. Difference in mean values was calculated between NSP2 tracts and each of the three comparison groups. * $p < 0.05$

Table 1:   County-level NSP2 expenditures and property outcomes

County	Jurisdictions	Grantees	NSP $ (mi)	Props	$/prop (000s)	CDBG hsg $ (mi)
Los Angeles CA	12	6	219.8	558	393.84	123.9
Cook IL	2	5	131.9	262	503.57	105.0
Maricopa AZ	7	2	114.7	493	232.66	25.9
Miami-Dade FL	6	2	89.9	295	304.88	27.2
Wayne MI	4	1	75.6	1947	38.84	50.7
Philadelphia PA	1	2	58.6	492	119.11	100.5
Cuyahoga OH	6	1	25.9	758	34.17	52.6
Total	38	19	716.5	4805	149.11	485.8

Notes: For count of jurisdictions, CDPs and unincorporated areas within the same county are counted together (falling under the county government). Grantees working under the same coalition in multiple counties (e.g. Habitat for Humanity, Chicanos Por La Causa) are treated as separate organizations. All monetary values shown in constant 2013 dollars.

Table 2:   County-level NSP2 activities

	REHAB/REDEV		DEMO/LB		FINANCE		MULTI	
	% prop	% spend	% prop	% spend	% prop	% spend	% prop	% spend
Sand States								
Miami-Dade FL	96.9	77.4	0.3	0.0	0.0	0.0	2.7	22.6
Maricopa AZ	95.7	98.4	0	0	0.0	0.0	4.3	1.6
Los Angeles CA	78.9	80.6	0	0	16.5	8.5	4.7	10.9
Other								
Cook IL	62.6	94.5	31.7	1.9	0.8	2.7	5.0	0.9
Philadelphia PA	41.7	85.9	56.9	6.8	0.0	0.0	1.4	7.3
Rust Belt								
Wayne MI	6.9	69.0	89.9	24.1	0.0	0.0	3.2	6.8
Cuyahoga OH	6.1	45.0	88.4	24.5	1.5	16.8	4.1	13.7

Notes: Rehabilitation and redevelopment activities are grouped together, as are demolition and land-banking. Properties that received financing in conjunction with either rehab or redevelopment are counted under rehab/redevelopment. Properties classified as MULTI received funding under two activity categories: rehab/redevelopment as well as demolition. It was unclear from grantee data whether there was a structure on the property following completion of NSP.

Table 3:   Tract-level NSP2 investments

County	Tracts	Properties	NSP2 $	$/prop	$/hsg value
Cook IL	44	4.0	1,874,157	324,221	9.66
Cuyahoga OH	89	6.0	104,509	9,872	1.36
Los Angeles CA	205	2.0	668,895	330,043	1.64
Maricopa AZ	113	2.0	268,610	148,112	1.85
Miami-Dade FL	56	2.0	399,996	131,659	1.84
Philadelphia PA	49	4.0	561,098	170,946	6.26
Wayne MI	92	14.0	130,450	8,652	2.13
Total	648	3.0	386,769	160,964	2.00

Notes: Median values per tract shown. $/hsg value is tract-level NSP2 expenditures divided by median housing value reported in 2005-2009 ACS. All monetary values shown in constant 2013 dollars.

Table 4: Variable definitions and sources

Variable	Definition	Source
NSP activity/treatment		
NSP2	=1 if at least one NSP2 property ever in tract, = 0 otherwise	Grantee data
NSP $/value	NSP2 expenditures/median housing value	Grantee data, ACS
Housing market outcomes		
Distress rate	properties in any stage of mortgage distress per 1000 housing units	Core Logic, ACS
Vacancy rate	vacancies per 1000 housing units	USPS, ACS
Sales	Number of arms' length housing sales/year (see appendix)	Core Logic
Price	median sales price of arms' length housing sales	Core Logic
Population and neighborhood characteristics		
Hsg value	median value of owner-occupied housing	ACS 2005-2009
Pop density	population density (per square mile)	
Low income	= 1 if tract median income < county median income, = 0 otherwise	
Hispanic	% Hispanic	
Black	% African American	
Hsg 1-4 fam	% housing units in 1-4 family properties	
Investor	% housing transactions purchased by non-owner-occupants	Core Logic
Dist CBD	miles from tract centroid to CBD (city hall)	Google maps
Hsg program	= 1 if NSP1, CDBG, HOME, or LIHTC; = 0 if none	HUD

Table 5   Baseline characteristics of NSP2 tracts

	Cook	Cuyahoga	LA	Maricopa	Miami	Philly	Wayne
Housing market outcomes (2009)							
Distress rate	20.30	37.23	77.66	129.71	68.80	17.68	53.25
Vacancy rate	207.38	142.32	29.15	140.36	77.87	52.04	225.92
Sales volume	16.02	18.15	47.89	145.27	33.09	36.29	34.17
Sales price (Core Logic 2009)	98,478	22,984	220,676	83,127	92,677	108,310	8,605
Hsg value (ACS 2005-09)	230,484	86,385	407,367	175,891	195,811	88,192	75,779
Targeting of investment							
Other hsg program	65.9%	96.6%	51.7%	70.8%	80.4%	71.4%	100.0%
Low income	95.5%	87.6%	67.8%	81.4%	78.6%	65.3%	88.0%
Other nhood characteristics (2005-09)							
Investor	71.67	67.91	42.36	64.42	57.73	45.97	73.43
Pop density	19,938	7,881	14,744	7,089	7,736	20,648	7,819
Black	53.37	62.04	18.05	7.08	64.55	67.70	80.96
Hispanic	37.12	7.90	65.05	54.81	29.68	13.14	1.13
Hsg 1-4 fam	67.39	76.33	70.51	71.91	60.43	20.94	80.99
Dist CBD	6.32	4.70	6.83	7.26	8.95	5.15	5.41

Table 6:   Predicting NSP2 tract selection

	Cook	Cuyahoga	LA	Maricopa	Miami	Philly	Wayne
ln(Distress rate)	-0.0041*	-0.134*	0.498***	-0.530**	0.052	0.0795***	0.095
	(0.002)	(0.075)	(0.173)	(0.261)	(0.294)	(0.027)	(0.076)
ln(Vacancy rate)	0.0079**	0.068	0.061	0.231**	0.081	-0.007	0.038
	(0.004)	(0.104)	(0.095)	(0.092)	(0.256)	(0.026)	(0.075)
ln(Sales)	0.0059**	-0.0738**	0.808***	0.511***	-0.009	0.019	0.009
	(0.002)	(0.033)	(0.143)	(0.118)	(0.190)	(0.048)	(0.062)
Hsg program	0.0106*	0.225***	0.237*	0.501***	1.069***	0.007	0.244***
	(0.006)	(0.080)	(0.136)	(0.126)	(0.281)	(0.029)	(0.037)
Low income	0.003	-0.015	-0.719***	0.733***	-0.344	-0.009	0.064
	(0.003)	(0.095)	(0.195)	(0.241)	(0.367)	(0.045)	(0.071)
Black	0.0004***	0.002	0.0318***	0.0573***	0.0280**	0.0019*	-0.0027**
	(0.000)	(0.002)	(0.006)	(0.014)	(0.013)	(0.001)	(0.001)
Hispanic	0.0006***	0.00439*	0.0298***	0.0202***	0.008	0.002	-0.0142***
	(0.000)	(0.002)	(0.005)	(0.005)	(0.011)	(0.001)	(0.003)
Pseudo R-sq	0.3106	0.1328	0.4769	0.3592	0.4561	0.2068	0.2
Observations	814	256	1,118	520	179	337	317

Results of probit model on binary outcome, whether tract ever received NSP2 investment. Robust standard errors, clustered by PUMA, in parentheses. Regression also include lagged changes in distress, vacancy and sales, median housing value, pop density, percent 1-4 family housing, distance to CBD, and place fixed effects. *** $p<0.01$, ** $p<0.05$, * $p<0.1$

Table 7: Change in distressed properties, 2009-2013

	(1)	(2)	(3)	(4)
NSP2 metric:	Any NSP2	ln(NSP$/value)		
Comparison group:	All non-NSP	All non-NSP	Hsg program	Low income
Cook				
NSP2	-0.033	-0.050	-0.036	-0.027
	(0.075)	(0.031)	(0.031)	(0.030)
Observations	810	810	253	493
R-squared	0.079	0.082	0.200	0.129
Cuyahoga				
NSP2	0.114**	0.045	0.043	0.046
	(0.046)	(0.031)	(0.031)	(0.034)
Observations	255	255	220	201
R-squared	0.240	0.226	0.268	0.243
LA				
NSP2	-0.005	-0.008	-0.015	-0.013
	(0.019)	(0.015)	(0.016)	(0.015)
Observations	1118	1118	478	746
R-squared	0.227	0.227	0.227	0.159
Maricopa				
NSP2	0.010	0.012	0.0177**	0.011
	(0.016)	(0.009)	(0.008)	(0.009)
Observations	520	520	306	303
R-squared	0.351	0.353	0.386	0.403
Miami				
NSP2	-0.025	0.010	0.021	0.023
	(0.032)	(0.014)	(0.017)	(0.015)
Observations	179	179	97	135
R-squared	0.341	0.340	0.461	0.425
Philly				
NSP2	-0.007	-0.002	0.001	-0.004
	(0.058)	(0.024)	(0.024)	(0.018)
Observations	333	333	195	182
R-squared	0.123	0.123	0.225	0.193
Wayne				
NSP2	-0.023	-0.004	-0.006	-0.012
	(0.031)	(0.018)	(0.018)	(0.020)
Observations	316	316	267	266
R-squared	0.302	0.301	0.325	0.316

Dependent variable is change in distressed properties, 2009-2013. Regressions include controls for baseline and lagged changes in distress, vacancy, sales volume; log of subsidized housing properties, median housing value, investor purchase share, population density, median household income, black and Hispanic shares, percent 1-4 family housing and distance to CBD. All regressions include PUMA fixed effects. Robust standard errors in parentheses. *** p<0.01, ** p<0.05, * p<0.1

Table 8: Change in vacant properties, 2009-2013

		(1)	(2)	(3)	(4)
NSP2 metric:		Any NSP2		ln(NSP$/value)	
Comparison		Non-NSP	Non-NSP	Hsg program	Low income
Cook					
	NSP2	0.168***	0.0589**	0.0424	0.0595**
		(0.058)	(0.024)	(0.027)	(0.024)
	Observations	814	814	255	495
	R-squared	0.331	0.329	0.411	0.323
Cuyahoga					
	NSP2	-0.110***	-0.0656**	-0.0649**	-0.0668**
		(0.041)	(0.027)	(0.027)	(0.030)
	Observations	256	256	221	202
	R-squared	0.41	0.406	0.437	0.398
LA					
	NSP2	0.0419	0.0258	0.0302	0.00644
		(0.051)	(0.039)	(0.049)	(0.042)
	Observations	1,118	1,118	478	746
	R-squared	0.513	0.513	0.522	0.527
Maricopa					
	NSP2	0.054	0.034	0.023	0.049
		(0.060)	(0.035)	(0.038)	(0.033)
	Observations	508	508	302	300
	R-squared	0.313	0.313	0.342	0.277
Miami					
	NSP2	-0.002	-0.010	-0.057	-0.006
		(0.082)	(0.036)	(0.040)	(0.038)
	Observations	179	179	97	135
	R-squared	0.5	0.5	0.524	0.5
Philly					
	NSP2	0.041	0.028	0.020	0.002
		(0.074)	(0.029)	(0.025)	(0.025)
	Observations	337	337	197	185
	R-squared	0.525	0.526	0.519	0.469
Wayne					
	NSP2	0.0654*	0.029	0.020	0.024
		(0.036)	(0.021)	(0.018)	(0.022)
	Observations	317	317	267	267
	R-squared	0.384	0.382	0.481	0.36

Dependent variable is change in vacant properties, 2009-2013. Regressions include controls for baseline and lagged changes in distress, vacancy, sales volume; log of subsidized housing properties, median housing value, investor purchase share, population density, median household income, black and Hispanic shares, percent 1-4 family housing and distance to CBD. All regressions include PUMA fixed effects. Robust standard errors in parentheses. *** $p<0.01$, ** $p<0.05$, * $p<0.1$

Table 9: Change in arms' length sale volume, 2009-2012

		(1)	(2)	(3)	(4)
NSP2 metric:		Any NSP2		ln(NSP$/value)	
Comparison		Non-NSP	Non-NSP	Hsg program	Low income
Cook					
	NSP2	0.109	0.0361	0.103**	0.0531
		(0.098)	(0.040)	(0.051)	(0.050)
	Observations	805	805	254	489
	R-squared	0.372	0.372	0.459	0.364
Cuyahoga					
	NSP2	0.152**	0.102**	0.0923**	0.117**
		(0.063)	(0.042)	(0.043)	(0.047)
	Observations	255	255	220	201
	R-squared	0.464	0.464	0.462	0.437
LA					
	NSP2	0.0653**	0.0582**	0.027	0.0512*
		(0.033)	(0.025)	(0.034)	(0.030)
	Observations	1,117	1,117	477	745
	R-squared	0.554	0.555	0.59	0.543
Maricopa					
	NSP2	0.056	0.021	0.009	0.003
		(0.035)	(0.020)	(0.020)	(0.023)
	Observations	519	519	306	303
	R-squared	0.688	0.687	0.671	0.667
Miami					
	NSP2	-0.092	-0.0597*	-0.0895**	-0.051
		(0.075)	(0.033)	(0.042)	(0.038)
	Observations	178	178	96	134
	R-squared	0.515	0.521	0.607	0.542
Philly					
	NSP2	0.068	0.034	0.038	0.037
		(0.069)	(0.028)	(0.032)	(0.037)
	Observations	337	337	197	185
	R-squared	0.375	0.376	0.423	0.398
Wayne					
	NSP2	0.113	0.031	0.042	0.058
		(0.083)	(0.048)	(0.050)	(0.057)
	Observations	316	316	266	266
	R-squared	0.288	0.284	0.336	0.315

Dependent variable is change in annual sales volume, 2009-2013. Regressions include controls for baseline and lagged changes in distress, vacancy, sales volume; log of subsidized housing properties, median housing value, investor purchase share, population density, median household income, black and Hispanic shares, percent 1-4 family housing and distance to CBD. All regressions include PUMA fixed effects. Robust standard errors in parentheses. *** $p<0.01$, ** $p<0.05$, * $p<0.1$

Appendix Table 1:   Distribution of NSP2 tract investments

	mean	median	sd	min	max	N
COOK						
Properties	6.0	4.0	7.5	1.0	39.0	44
NSP2 $	2,998,535	1,874,157	3,623,086	8,248	17,300,000	44
$/prop	1,118,219	324,221	2,804,974	8,248	17,300,000	44
$/hsg value	12.74	9.66	12.80	0.04	58.06	44
CUYAHOGA						
Properties	8.5	6.0	10.2	1.0	64.0	89
NSP2 $	290,984	104,509	668,008	425	4,150,778	89
$/prop	43,036	9,872	101,747	425	830,156	89
$/hsg value	3.67	1.36	8.90	0.00	59.17	88
LA						
Properties	2.7	2.0	2.2	1.0	15.0	205
NSP2 $	1,072,004	668,895	1,606,715	48,305	12,600,000	205
$/prop	531,182	330,043	1,350,758	24,153	12,600,000	205
$/hsg value	2.54	1.64	3.35	0.11	26.24	203
MARICOPA						
Properties	4.4	2.0	7.0	1.0	44.0	113
NSP2 $	1,015,069	268,610	2,016,017	43,385	13,800,000	113
$/prop	354,038	148,112	939,456	38,123	6,923,563	113
$/hsg value	5.91	1.85	13.07	0.28	98.49	113
MIAMI						
Properties	5.3	2.0	12.1	1.0	87.0	56
NSP2 $	1,606,038	399,996	2,340,022	3,484	9,843,135	56
$/prop	650,716	131,659	1,168,183	3,484	5,418,138	56
$/hsg value	9.81	1.84	15.43	0.02	69.86	55
PHILLY						
Properties	10.0	4.0	18.7	1.0	124.0	49
NSP2 $	1,195,500	561,098	1,584,833	12,574	6,141,603	49
$/prop	235,497	170,946	643,865	8,636	4,593,716	49
$/hsg value	15.99	6.26	24.37	0.12	121.20	49
WAYNE						
Properties	21.2	14.0	21.9	1.0	109.0	92
NSP2 $	822,014	130,450	2,494,971	5,438	20,500,000	92
$/prop	33,138	8,652	82,381	5,086	640,675	92
$/hsg value	6.98	2.13	14.53	0.04	82.65	91

Appendix Table 2:   Variable summary statistics, all counties and tracts

Variable	Mean	St Dev	Min	Max	n
NSP activity/treatment					
NSP2	0.18	0.38	0.00	1.00	3600
NSP $/value	1.12	5.94	0.00	121.20	3600
Housing market outcomes					
Distress rate	42.98	41.32	0.00	395.14	3600
Vacancy rate	83.55	118.93	0.00	4,509.32	3600
Sales	43.94	92.17	0.00	2,134.00	3600
Price	225,409	215,519	2,040	2,123,882	2879
Population and neighborhood characteristics					
Hsg value	316,601	231,576	6,800	1,200,000	3600
Pop density	12,833	10,007	2	91,796	3600
Low income	0.62	0.49	0.00	1.00	3600
Hispanic	30.86	31.46	0.00	100.00	3600
Black	29.90	36.65	0.00	100.00	3600
Hsg 1-4 fam	60.69	28.03	0.00	100.00	3600
Investor	51.79	20.80	0.00	100.00	3600
Dist CBD	6.07	3.87	0.01	56.82	3600
Hsg program	0.46	0.50	0.00	1.00	3600

Appendix Table 3:   Right-hand side coefficients, change in distressed properties

Dep variable:	Change in distressed properties (2009-2013)						
County:	Cook	Cuyahoga	LA	Maricopa	Miami	Philly	Wayne
ln(NSP$/value)	-0.050	0.045	-0.008	0.012	0.010	-0.002	-0.004
	(0.031)	(0.031)	(0.015)	(0.009)	(0.014)	(0.024)	(0.018)
ln(Distress rate)	-0.173***	-0.164***	-0.0770***	-0.0964***	-0.164***	-0.123***	-0.225***
	(0.034)	(0.060)	(0.017)	(0.015)	(0.039)	(0.040)	(0.038)
ln(Vacancy rate)	-0.034	-0.074	-0.004	0.005	-0.0723***	0.0553*	-0.0971**
	(0.029)	(0.050)	(0.009)	(0.007)	(0.024)	(0.030)	(0.038)
ln(Hsg value)	-0.118*	-0.028	0.000	0.012	-0.091	-0.082	0.040
	(0.060)	(0.082)	(0.027)	(0.016)	(0.061)	(0.071)	(0.044)
ln(Sales)	0.109***	0.0784*	0.0306**	0.005	0.0826***	0.017	0.101***
	(0.025)	(0.045)	(0.013)	(0.009)	(0.025)	(0.039)	(0.031)
Investor	0.000	-0.002	-0.00149***	0.000	0.001	-0.002	0.00555***
	(0.001)	(0.002)	(0.001)	(0.001)	(0.001)	(0.002)	(0.002)
Distress change 06-09	0.005	-0.194***	-0.0626**	-0.0908***	-0.023	-0.010	0.114***
	(0.034)	(0.053)	(0.025)	(0.034)	(0.051)	(0.032)	(0.038)
Vacancy change 06-09	0.0661*	0.011	-0.002	-0.006	0.005	-0.041	0.121***
	(0.037)	(0.076)	(0.009)	(0.010)	(0.026)	(0.043)	(0.041)
Sales change 06-09	-0.0994***	0.036	-0.014	-0.028	-0.049	-0.0925*	-0.108***
	(0.034)	(0.052)	(0.015)	(0.018)	(0.035)	(0.053)	(0.039)
ln(Housing properties)	-0.028	-0.0497*	0.010	0.003	0.015	-0.009	-0.0464**
	(0.038)	(0.026)	(0.013)	(0.013)	(0.023)	(0.035)	(0.019)
ln(Income)	0.006	-0.122*	0.0925***	-0.004	-0.022	-0.028	0.110**
	(0.055)	(0.072)	(0.029)	(0.030)	(0.062)	(0.081)	(0.045)
ln(Pop density)	-0.0919***	0.018	-0.0199*	0.0125*	-0.026	0.010	-0.034
	(0.029)	(0.039)	(0.011)	(0.007)	(0.025)	(0.040)	(0.028)
Black	0.00224*	0.000	0.00140**	0.00228*	-0.002	0.000	0.00151*
	(0.001)	(0.001)	(0.001)	(0.001)	(0.002)	(0.001)	(0.001)
Hispanic	0.00274**	-0.002	0.001	-0.001	-0.003	-0.00407**	0.002
	(0.001)	(0.003)	(0.000)	(0.001)	(0.002)	(0.002)	(0.001)
Hsg 1-4 fam	0.000	0.001	0.000	0.00121***	0.00135**	0.000	0.001
	(0.001)	(0.002)	(0.000)	(0.000)	(0.001)	(0.002)	(0.001)
ln(Dist CBD)	0.033	0.014	-0.009	0.003	0.048	0.095	-0.034
	(0.086)	(0.104)	(0.027)	(0.019)	(0.072)	(0.133)	(0.068)
PUMA fixed effects	Y	Y	Y	Y	Y	Y	Y
Observations	810	255	1,118	520	179	333	316
R-squared	0.082	0.226	0.227	0.353	0.34	0.123	0.301

Dependent variable is change in distressed properties, 2009-2013. Regressions include all census tracts. Robust standard errors in parentheses. *** p<0.01, ** p<0.05, * p<0.1

Appendix Table 4:   Count of tracts with 10+ arms' length sales in 2009 and 2012

	Any NSP2		Housing program		Low income		All tracts	
	All tracts	10+ sales	All tracts	10+ sales	All tracts	10+ sales	All tracts	10+ sales
Cook	44	18	218	96	507	178	882	455
Cuyahoga	89	46	143	71	138	49	282	144
Los Angeles	205	196	298	207	589	406	1,170	965
Maricopa	113	111	205	197	207	177	558	521
Miami	56	49	43	36	82	73	182	164
Philly	49	35	151	102	158	76	381	246
Wayne	92	61	185	115	193	105	337	215

Appendix Table 5:   Change in median sales price, 2009-2012

	Cuyahoga	LA	Maricopa	Miami	Philly	Wayne
Any NSP2	-0.005	0.017	-0.028	0.025	0.027	-0.034
	(0.083)	(0.021)	(0.023)	(0.063)	(0.049)	(0.086)
ln(NSP$/value)	0.011	0.018	-0.0256*	0.017	0.016	-0.016
	(0.052)	(0.017)	(0.013)	(0.027)	(0.021)	(0.046)
R-squared	0.417	0.237	0.522	0.276	0.270	0.167
Observations	144	963	521	164	246	215

Dependent variable is change in sales price, 2009-2012. Regressions include controls for baseline and lagged changes in distress, vacancy, sales volume; log of subsidized housing properties, median housing value, investor purchase share, population density, median household income, black and Hispanic shares, percent 1-4 family housing and distance to CBD. All regressions include PUMA fixed effects. Robust standard errors in parentheses. *** $p<0.01$, ** $p<0.05$, * $p<0.1$

www.ingramcontent.com/pod-product-compliance
Lightning Source LLC
Chambersburg PA
CBHW080614180526
45168CB00007B/2915